THE PARANORMAL THROUGHOUT HISTORY

GHOSTS AND POLTERGEISTS IN HISTORY

ANITA CROY

rosen publishing's rosen central
New York

Published in 2020 by The Rosen Publishing Group, Inc.
29 East 21st Street
New York, NY 10010

First Edition

Produced for Rosen by Calcium Creative Ltd
Editors for Calcium: Sarah Eason and Tim Cooke
Designer: Paul Myerscough and Jessica Moon
Picture researcher: Rachel Blount

Photo credits: Cover: Shutterstock: Elena Schweitzer; Inside: Library of Congress: George Grantham Bain Collection: p. 38; Shutterstock: Artfully Photographer: pp. 4–5; Orhan Cam: pp. 32–33; Alex Cherepanov: p. 35b; Everett Historical: p. 31; Jonson: pp. 12–13; Kamira: p. 5c; Brenda Kean: p. 6; Kzenon: p. 37; Sarunyu L: p. 36; Zacarias Pereira da Mata: p. 15; Ray49: p. 41; Thatsmymop: p. 33b; Lario Tus: p. 43; Wikimedia Commons: pp. 8–9, 26, 27, 34–35t; Clark Bell: p. 28; Boissard, Jean-Jaques; Bry, Theodor d: p. 16; Currier and Ives: p. 30; Alphonse de Neuville or A. Jahandier: p. 23t; G. W. Edmondson: p. 18; Henry Fuseli: pp. 22–23; Friedrich Wilhelm Heine (1845–1921): p. 13tr; M. V. Ingram: p. 20; Internet Archive Book Images: p. 11t; John Wesley Jarvis. Harris Brisbane Dick Fund, 1964: p. 21; John Leech: pp. 1, 25; William Lefroy: p. 14; Elie Marcuse: pp. 10–11; W. J. Morgan & Co. Lith. Of Cleveland, Ohio: p. 17; William H. Mumler: p. 42; Marie-Lan Nguyen: pp. 3, 7; John Quidor: p. 24; B. A. Rolfe Productions: p. 39.

Cataloging-in-Publication Data

Names: Croy, Anita.
Title: Ghosts and poltergeists in history / Anita Croy.
Description: New York : Rosen Central, 2020. | Series: The paranormal throughout history | Includes glossary and index.
Identifiers: ISBN 9781725346635 (pbk.) | ISBN 9781725346574 (library bound)
Subjects: LCSH: Ghosts—Juvenile literature. | Poltergeists—Juvenile literature. | Haunted places—Juvenile literature.
Classification: LCC BF1461.C79 2020 | DDC 133.1—dc23

Manufactured in the United States of America

Cover: For centuries, people have claimed that they have been visited by departed souls in the form of ghosts.

CONTENTS

CHAPTER 1

THE EARLIEST GHOSTS

For people who believe in ghosts, these spirits are the souls of the dead who appear to the living. They are thought to exist in a parallel world from where they come back to our world. Why they do that—and whether they really exist—are questions that remain unanswered.

Ghosts are usually said to haunt old or spooky buildings, as a photographer has imagined in this image.

Talking of Ghosts

The eighteenth-century English writer Dr. Samuel Johnson observed: "Talking of ghosts, it is wonderful that 5,000 years have now elapsed since the creation of the world, and still it is undecided whether or not there has ever been an instance [example] of the spirit of any person appearing after death. All argument is against it, but all belief is for it." Dr. Johnson's words could have been spoken today. In a 2003 poll, 51 percent of Americans said that they believed in ghosts.

An Ancient Belief

The word ghost comes from a Saxon word of the Middle Ages, *gaste*, which means guest, but ghosts have been around since earliest times. During the Neolithic, or Stone Age, humans buried the dead with special ceremonies to make sure their souls did not return to haunt the living.

The ancient Egyptians also believed their dead had to be buried carefully to ensure they would pass into the afterlife. If funeral rituals were not followed correctly, the soul of the dead person could not cross the River Styx to reach the afterlife. Instead, it would wander Earth in misery.

The appearance of ghosts was recorded by the early Babylonians using images and cuneiform, the first form of writing, on clay tablets.

The Evil Dead

The Assyrians lived in what are now northern Iraq and Turkey from around 2500 BCE. They were among the first people to believe that ghosts could be good or evil. They used specific words to describe evil spirits, who wanted to do harm to people. The Assyrians believed evil spirits were the ghosts of people who had been left unburied or who had not been buried properly.

THE CLASSICAL WORLD

The ancient Greeks and the Romans, who later took over much of the Greeks' territory, both believed the souls of the dead wandered the Earth. These ghosts haunted people who were bad, frightened good people, and generally meddled in everyday life.

Name for the Spirits

The Greeks and Romans had different names for spirits. The ghosts of those who had led good lives were called *lares*, while those who had led bad lives were known as *larvae* or *lemures*. The spirits of the dead were deified, or given the status of gods, and were known as *dii manes*. Engraved on the tombstones in Roman burial grounds was D.M. or D.M.S., which stood for *Dis Manibus* or *Dis Manibus Sacrum*, which meant "Sacred to the Manes Gods." The Romans offered sacrifices to these ghost gods.

Romans kept altars in their homes where they prayed to the *lares*, the ghosts of the dead.

An Ancient Ghost Story

The Roman writer Pliny recorded a famous Greek ghost story. A ghost haunted a house in Athens, and dragged a heavy chain as it wandered through the building at night. A philosopher called Athenodorus rented the house and decided to silence the ghost. One night, he followed the ghost, which pointed to a spot in the courtyard of the house before it vanished. The next day, Athenodorus ordered the spot to be dug up. The hole revealed the skeleton of a man wrapped in chains. Athenodorus had the skeleton burned and the ghost was never seen again.

When they held festivals to honor the *lemuria*, Romans burned black beans over the graves and beat drums to drive away any ghosts that might be lingering around.

The Odyssey

The Greek poet Homer composed his epic poem, *The Odyssey*, around 725–675 BCE. It was written down centuries later. Homer tells the story of Ulysses's 10-year journey home after the Trojan War, which is thought to be based on a real event that took place in about 1250 BCE. During his voyages, Ulysses has several encounters with ghosts, including those of the warriors Achilles, Ajax, and Agamemnon in Hades, or the underworld.

Homer describes ghosts as being like the people they were in life.

AROUND THE WORLD

The idea that a soul lives on after a person has died is one believed by people many cultures across the world. For many ancient cultures, honoring the dead and ghosts was a vital part of everyday life. They believed that ghosts came into being because of various causes, which were often connected with being buried incorrectly. That was one reason why ancient peoples took such care when burying the dead.

In ancient China, people believed that ghosts were a result of a bad or painful death. Somebody who had drowned or died in battle might become a ghost, for example. They could only be seen at night by torchlight. The Chinese belief in ghosts was, and still is, influenced by their belief in ancestor worship. The Chinese believe their ancestors shape their lives on Earth, so they honor them after death. Failing to honor the ancestors correctly creates so-called hungry ghosts, who torment the living.

This Chinese drawing from a scroll, or long roll of paper, shows "hungry ghosts" making mischief among the living.

The Ghost Festival

The ancient Chinese honored their dead during the Ghost Festival, which was held on the 15 day of the seventh lunar month. This marked the time the Chinese believed the veil between the worlds of the living and the dead was at its thinnest, so the dead could easily cross over.

The Ghost Festival is still celebrated today. It is similar to the Day of the Dead celebrated in Latin America on November 1 and 2, and the Celtic Samhain festival from ancient Europe, when dead spirits were said to walk the Earth. As part of all these festivals, the living leave food and gifts for the dead.

Ancient India's Bhoots

Like the Chinese, the ancient Indians believed it was vital to keep the ancestors happy. The dead had to be dealt with according to strict guidelines. If any guideline was broken, the dead might come back to haunt the living. Known as *bhoots*, the ghosts appeared in human form but were given away because their feet appeared to be backward. That was a sign that something had gone wrong, so the dead spirit was not in a good place. The ancient Indians believed that the bhoots roamed the Earth looking for a living body to inhabit. Some people think that the practice of cremation, or burning dead bodies, started because it was a way of preventing the spirit from returning to Earth.

CHAPTER 2

MEDIEVAL GHOSTS

During the Middle Ages from about 500 to 1500, the Christian Church dominated every part of people's lives. Ghosts played an important part in Christian teaching. The Church said they were spirits who had become stuck in purgatory, which was an unpleasant place where the dead waited to go to heaven. The only way these souls could reach heaven was if the living paid for prayers to be said for their souls.

Ghosts in the Bible

Ghosts are mentioned in the Bible. The most famous ghost story appears in the Book of Samuel in the Old Testament. According to the story, King Saul of Israel was worried about the outcome if he fought the Philistines. He called a magician, who summoned up the ghost of the prophet Samuel. The ghost warned the king that he would be defeated, but Saul went into battle anyway. The prediction came true, and the king killed himself on the battlefield.

Here, King Saul prepares to kill himself after the Israelites are defeated in battle by the Philistines.

This drawing illustrates the Church's idea that the world was full of threats sent by the Devil to corrupt Christians.

The Devil's Work

The Church used the idea of ghosts or spirits to make Christians afraid. The idea that the souls of the dead could torture the living helped the Church extend its influence over people. The Church taught that only God could perform the miracle of resurrection, or bringing the dead back to life, as Jesus had shown his followers when he raised Lazarus's body. It followed that ghosts, therefore, must be the work of the Devil. The Devil could possess the living, people believed, so they reasoned he must also be able to possess the dead and use them for his own evil purposes. According to the Church, there was no limit to the different forms that the Devil could assume—including that of ghosts.

Between Life and Death

Medieval science suggested there was a brief period between the moment of death and the soul's departure from the body when a corpse was easy prey for the Devil. Once the body started to decay, the Devil could no longer influence it. But if the Devil turned a corpse into the walking dead, there was no limit to the nighttime harm the ghost might perform.

A SPIRIT ARMY

One popular medieval folktale told the story of the ancient British King Herla. Herla is destined to spend eternity wandering Earth after making a pact with an evil spirit called the Dwarf King. Herla and his followers rode endlessly on their horses, because if they dismounted they would turn to dust. The spirits were known as Hellequin's Army.

Ghost Army

On a January night in 1091, a priest named Walchelin was making his way home in Normandy, France, when he heard a great crowd approaching. Walchelin was frightened that it might be an invading army, so he hid behind a tree. He watched as thousands of people passed by. First came hundreds of peasants carrying their worldly possessions. Hundreds of women followed on horseback. As they bounced up and down, red hot nails in their saddles burned and stabbed their skin. Next came hundreds of members of the clergy, followed by a crowd of knights.

Walchelin reported meeting the ghost army by moonlight on a lonely country road.

As Walchelin watched the army go past, he began to recognize some of the people. They were all people who had died in recent years.

The Wandering Dead

Finally, Walchelin saw his own brother, whom he had not seen for many years. Now the priest realized this was the fabled army of the dead. All these walking dead had committed sins when they were alive for which they were now being punished with eternal restlessness. Walchelin spoke to his brother, who told him that he could only be released from his eternal wandering if Walchelin paid the Church for prayers to be said on his behalf.

Many European legends included stories of a wild hunt, in which the spirits of the dead rode through the skies.

Money for the Church

Paying for a mass to be said for the soul of the dead was a good way for the Church to raise money, and it was actively encouraged by priests. The Church taught that the soul could only be released from purgatory once prayers had been said for the soul. Then, and only then, could the soul make it to heaven.

MEDIEVAL GHOST STORIES

Around 1400 CE, a monk living at Byland Abbey in Yorkshire, England, used the last few empty pages of a book he had been copying out to write 12 scary ghost stories he had been told. The stories still survive. See if you find them as frightening as the monk who wrote them down.

In the stories, the dead rise from their graves and walk around at night, scaring the local villagers and dogs. One ghost gradually takes on human form and helps a man carry a sack of beans. In another story, a ghost appears to a tailor and asks him to persuade the priest to say prayers for the ghost's soul. Another story tells of a man buried at Byland Abbey whose ghost wanders the community, harming people. The monks decide to dig up his body and throw it in a lake, after which the hauntings stop.

Byland Abbey became a ruin after it was abandoned during the 1500s.

Ever since medieval times, ghosts have been said to be able to find rest with the help of the Church.

The Waking Dead

One ghost in the stories confesses to crimes he committed while alive, such as stealing from his master. In another story, a local man manages to grab hold of a ghost and keep hold of him until the local priest arrives in the graveyard. The priest calls upon the Holy Trinity and Jesus Christ to conjure up the ghost. Once the ghost appears, he speaks not from his mouth but from deep inside him. The men learn that, when he was alive, the ghost committed sins for which he was not forgiven. The priest hears the ghost's confession, and the spirit is finally able to rest.

Byland Ghost Story

In one Byland Abbey ghost story, a spirit appeared three nights in a row, calling out to a man named William. On the fourth night, William was walking with his dog when he heard a terrifying shout. The shout came again, much closer, and the dog ran between William's legs to hide. Suddenly, a spirit appeared right in front of them. Calling upon the Lord and Jesus Christ, William charged at the spirit, telling it to depart. The spirit unfurled like a piece of cloth and sailed into the midnight sky.

CHAPTER 3

TROUBLEMAKING GHOSTS

In the 1500s, people's views of ghosts began to change. Rather than believing it was possible to get rid of ghosts by paying the Church to say prayers, some people decided that ghosts were messengers from hell who tried to trap people into committing sins on Earth. This view was summed up in 1569 in a book called *Of Ghostes and Spirites Walking by Nyght*.

A Stage Ghost

Toward the end of the 1500s, William Shakespeare put a ghost at the center of *Hamlet*. The play tells the story of the Danish prince Hamlet, who takes revenge on his uncle, who has killed his father, the King of Denmark. The prince only knows that his father has been murdered because his father's ghost comes back to tell him.

John Dee was part scientist and part magician. He believed it was possible to speak to the dead.

At the top right of this poster for an 1884 production of *Hamlet*, the prince meets his father's ghost.

Talking to the Dead

John Dee was an Elizabethan scientist and philosopher. He is famous for his attempts to talk to angels using a crystal ball, with his assistant Edward Kelley acting as his medium, or go-between. Kelley himself was more interested in getting rich quick. One night, he dug up the just-buried corpse of a rich man and used various magic spells to try to get the body to reveal where the dead man had hidden his fortune.

Body Snatchers

When Edward Kelley dug up the dead body, he was committing what people saw as a serious crime. The dead were meant to be able to rest in peace. Disturbing their corpses also disturbed their spirits. In the 1800s, body snatching became more common. Doctors were exploring human anatomy, and needed bodies to cut open. Body snatchers, or resurrection men, secretly dug up the recently dead and sold them to the doctors.

MAKING MISCHIEF

In the eighteenth century, poltergeists were prevalent. Poltergeist is a German word meaning "noisy ghost," referring to their habit of moving furniture and generally making a nuisance of themselves. There were many examples of poltergeists in England, from the Cock Lane ghost that took London by storm in the 1760s to the ghost at the home of John Wesley, who became the founder of Methodism.

A poltergeist was said to disturb the Old Rectory at Epworth in Lincolnshire, England, between 1716 and 1717. The spirit, known as Old Jeffrey, was very noisy: it ran around and even blew musical horns. The haunting was notable because the rectory was the home of the Wesley family, including young John. After 1738, John Wesley would found the Methodist Church.

The Old Rectory at Epworth is now a museum owned by the British Methodist Church.

Also known as the Epworth Poltergeist, Old Jeffrey was said to have disturbed Wesley's younger sister, Hetty, in bed and to have made groaning noises that could be heard all over the house. Wesley believed the poltergeist was real and later wrote about it in his diary. He even wrote that people who did not believe in ghosts might as well not believe the Bible.

The Cock Lane Ghost

Even more famous than Old Jeffrey was the Cock Lane ghost, which plagued a house on Cock Lane in London in the 1760s. The spirit made rapping and scratching noises, terrifying a young girl who lived in the house named Elizabeth Parsons. She said she had seen a "shrouded figure without hands." The ghost was so famous that the house attracted many visitors, including the king's brother, the Duke of York. Large crowds gathered outside, hoping to hear the ghost making its knocking noises. The ghost was so popular it later made an appearance in Charles Dickens' novels.

A Possible Explanation

The ghost that haunted Cock Lane was said to be the spirit of Fanny Kent, the late wife of the house's tenant, William Kent. She had likely died of the disease smallpox, but people gossiped that William had murdered Fanny for her money. In fact, the authorities suspected Elizabeth Parsons was to blame for the knocking noises. They carried out an experiment in which they watched her sleep for two nights. There was no knocking on those nights, so they decided that the girl was indeed guilty.

THE BELL WITCH

The most famous nineteenth-century ghost in the United States was the Bell Witch of Tennessee. Between 1817 and 1821, it carried out a campaign of terror against the Bell family of Robertson County that ended in tragedy. The mystery of the spirit has never been solved.

AUTHENTICATED HISTORY

OF THE

BELL WITCH

And Other Stories of the World's Greatest Unexplained Phenomenon.

BY

M. V. INGRAM.

The first full-length description of the hauntings was published in 1894 by a newspaper editor.

Strange Events

In 1817, farmer John Bell was out in his field when he saw a strange animal with the body of a dog and the head of a rabbit. After that, all kinds of strange events happened at the family's farmhouse. There were rapping and scratching sounds, and covers were pulled off beds. The family's teenage daughter, Betsy, was slapped and pinched by an invisible attacker. Then the spirit started to sing hymns and recite sermons.

Over the next three years, the haunting got worse and worse. Finally, in 1820, John Bell's health could take it no more and he died. The spirit claimed it had poisoned him. In 1821, the spirit returned to Bell's widow, Lucy, to tell her it would return in seven years. It did, this time mainly haunting John Bell's son, John Bell Jr. When the spirit finally left, it swore it would return in 107 years' time.

A President's Visit

The Bell family's haunting attracted a lot of interest, including from Major General Andrew Jackson, a leading military commander who would later become US president. He visited the Bells intending to expose the story as a fraud. However, when his carriage mysteriously became stuck outside the farm, Jackson believed it was the poltergeist that had stopped it. A "witch tamer" traveling with Jackson threatened to shoot the ghost with a silver bullet—and the spirit kicked him out of the house. Jackson's men were so badly scared that the whole party fled.

An Unexplained Mystery

This time, the prediction did not come true, but the mystery of Bell Farm has never been explained. Some people said the trouble was caused by a witch named Kate Batts, who was in a fight with John Bell over money. Others said it was the spirit of a dead slave overseer, while others claimed that there was no poltergeist, and the events had all been caused in some way by Betsy Bell.

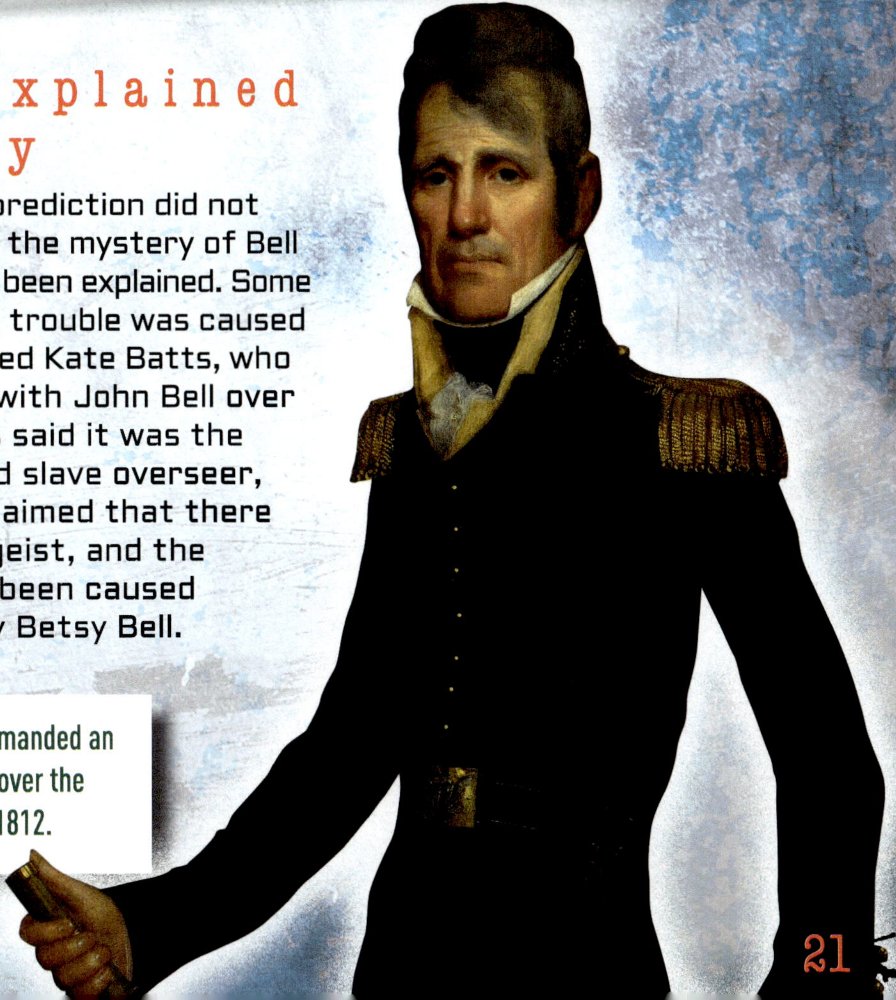

Andrew Jackson commanded an important US victory over the British in the War of 1812.

CHAPTER 4

THE GOTHIC AGE

The late eighteenth and early nineteenth centuries saw a great interest in the supernatural, or things, like ghosts, that could not be explained by reason. This movement was called the Gothic. Soon, many artists and writers used the supernatural in their works.

Monster Stories

In 1818, Mary Shelley published her novel *Frankenstein*. It told of a monster given life by a scientist in an experiment. The story was born out of an evening Shelley spent discussing ghosts in a dark room while a storm raged outside. Her novel struck a chord with the public, whose thirst for the Gothic was at its height. Also present at the spooky evening was Dr. Polidori, a physician. Polidori was also inspired to write a horror story. His story, *The Vampyre*, was the inspiration for Bram Stoker's famous novel *Dracula* (1897), the tale of the blood-sucking vampire Count Dracula.

Spirits in Art

It was not only writers who were interested in supernatural events. Painters such as the Swiss-born Henry Fuseli also imagined supernatural events.

Theater audiences were thrilled by phantasmagorias in which ghosts and spirits seemed to come alive.

Fuseli depicted a world in which evil spirits preyed on people. In his painting *The Changeling* (1780), a mother is shown recoiling in horror when she discovers a witch has stolen her baby and left a monster in the crib. Fuseli's most famous painting, *The Nightmare* (1782), was reproduced as a print so that as many people as possible could see the frightening image of an imp crouching over a sleeping woman, which seems to embody the terror of a nightmare.

Henry Fuseli's painting *The Nightmare* suggested the power of the imagination to create disturbing spirits.

Phantasmagorias

A phantasmagoria was a popular kind of horror theater that used tricks to scare the audience. Devices known as magic lanterns projected images of ghosts, demons, and skeletons on to walls, clouds of smoke, and semi-transparent screens. The use of mobile projectors and special sound effects left audiences terrified.

THE GHOST STORY

Everyone loves a scary ghost story, and in the 1900s such stories became a central fixture of popular entertainment. Ever since Shakespeare's *Hamlet* put a ghost on the stage, people had enjoyed being scared. In Britain, families told each other ghost stories on Christmas Eve.

A Hungry Audience

In the United States, one of the first ghost stories was "The Legend of Sleepy Hollow," written in 1820 by Washington Irving. Based on an earlier German story, it told of a headless horseman, who was said to be a German soldier who lost his head in battle. Later writers also wrote ghost stories, including famous authors such as Edgar Allen Poe and Edith Wharton. In 1898, Henry James wrote *The Turn of the Screw*, a short novel about the haunting of a governess and the children she is looking after. Many of these stories were later turned into movies.

The headless horseman of "The Legend of Sleepy Hollow" was said to have been a German soldier from the American Revolution.

A Christmas Carol

Probably the most famous of all nineteenth-century ghost stories was Charles Dickens' *A Christmas Carol*, which is still one of the most popular stories ever written. Dickens produced the novel in serial form just before Christmas 1843. In the story, Ebenezer Scrooge is visited by ghosts from Christmases in the past, present, and future and he learns the error of his mean ways. The ghosts teach him that he must learn to appreciate other people and to be more generous. Unlike the scary ghosts of other stories, these ghosts teach a lesson.

At the start of *A Christmas Carol*, Scrooge is visited by the ghost of his dead partner, Jacob Marley.

Causing Hallucinations

The rise in the popularity of ghost stories happened as the United States and Britain became more industrial countries. It may have had a physical cause, too. The gas lamps that were increasingly common in the streets and at home gave off a gas called carbon monoxide, which is now known to cause hallucinations. Add this to a world of foggy nights, dark rooms, and the fashion for ghost stories, and it is no surprise that imaginations ran riot with stories of supernatural hauntings.

GHOSTS IN THE NEWS

In the 1800s, newspapers carried many reports of hauntings to satisfy the public's interest in the supernatural. Mediums, who claimed to be able to communicate between the living and the dead, were famous celebrities. Every fashionable person wanted to take part in a séance, which was a meeting to try to talk to the dead.

Popular Stories

Popular publications often included accounts of ghosts and mysterious sightings for a readership that could not get enough of the stories. In 1877, the *New York Times* reported a haunting in Ohio under the headline "Queer Antics in a Staid Quaker Family's Pantry and Parlor." Newspapers covered stories of haunted railroad tunnels, headless ghosts, and strange apparitions. One newspaper sent out reporters throughout Illinois and Missouri looking for people who had seen ghosts. Most accounts reported sightings of ghosts as if they were real.

One popular character in nineteenth-century stories was Spring Heeled Jack, a mischievous spirit said to be capable of huge leaps.

The *Illustrated Police News* created a sensation with dramatic drawings of crimes and supernatural horrors.

Toll Hut Terror

One popular ghost story appeared in the *Illustrated Police News* in Britain in 1879. A toll-keeper had been murdered, and every year on the anniversary of his death, his ghost appeared at his old toll hut. This terrified travelers stopping at the hut to pay the fee to use the highway. They were so disturbed by the ghost that they stopped using the highway altogether. The highway and the hut fell into disrepair, which added to the ghostly impact of the illustrations in the newspaper of the ghost haunting his former, abandoned toll hut.

Terrified Teens

Many ghosts stories were about lone travelers on empty highways. In Woolwich in London, England, however, hundreds of boys claimed to see a ghost that haunted the grounds of the local church and school. The boys threw stones at the spirit, breaking several windows in the process. It was later discovered that the ghost was, in fact, a real person dressed up in white!

CHAPTER 5
A FASHION FOR GHOSTS

The second half of the nineteenth century was a boom time for those who believed in ghosts. It was also a time of growing scientific knowledge and skepticism, or doubting the truth of claims. Some people decided to approach ghosts and the supernatural using scientific study.

Search for Proof

In 1882, a group of people in London formed a society to investigate reports of paranormal activities. They wanted to see if there was any scientific proof for their existence. The Society of Psychical Research set out to investigate ghosts, extra sensory perception (ESP), and visions. It was the world's first society devoted to investigating the paranormal using scientific methods. Its members, which included a future prime minister of the United Kingdom, were determined not to be misled by tricks and fakes.

Thomas Jay Hudson was a leading investigator into supernatural phenomena.

The Committee for Skeptical Inquiry

Founded in 1976, in New York State, the Committee for Skeptical Inquiry, or CSI, is an organization that seeks to prove paranormal activity exists using scientific techniques. It tries to measure ghostly phenomena. Although it says it has evidence the spirit world exists, it has been unable to produce enough proof to convince others.

Finding Facts and Fakes

In order to examine whether paranormal phenomena did exist, members of the society first had to collect factual data to analyze. That meant sitting in on séances in which mediums claimed to connect the living with the dead or visiting haunted houses to see if resident ghosts appeared. Volunteers collected more than 700 personal accounts of paranormal activity, which were reproduced in two volumes, *Phantasms of the Living* (1886). More research resulted in the *Census of Hallucinations*. This was the largest-ever survey of its kind. Published in 1894, it asked 17,000 ordinary people if they had seen any kind of ghosts or paranormal hallucinations: 1,684 said they had. That was nearly 10 percent of those surveyed.

Members of the society spent much of their time exposing fake phenomena, such as mediums who conjured up "ghosts" using trickery and special effects. The society's members wanted to expose frauds, but they also hoped also to go on to show that some paranormal phenomena really do exist. Today, the society continues to try to prove the existence of ghosts—although it has not managed to do so yet.

CIVIL WAR GHOSTS

The Civil War (1861–1865) left around 620,000 Americans dead. Thousands of men were left unburied on the many battlefields, and soon stories began to circulate about ghosts haunting the battle sites. They were the spirits of young Union and Confederate soldiers who had died in the conflict.

The Ghosts of Gettysburg

The Battle of Gettysburg fought between July 1 and 3, 1863, in Pennsylvania, was the largest battle of the war. Around 50,000 men were killed, the largest number of casualties of the entire conflict. Several sites on and around the battlefield are said to be haunted. They include the Devil's Den, the name given to an area covered by large boulders. This was the site of fighting on the second day of the battle, when up to 20,000 men died.

The fighting at Gettysburg was some of the most intense during the Civil War.

One ghost is a barefooted man who walks about the Devil's Den wearing a floppy hat and a bright shirt. This was the uniform of an army unit from Texas. The ghost is said to mutter over and over, "What you're looking for is over there." No one knows what he is talking about.

Other Haunted Sites

The sites of less well-known battles are also haunted by victims of the war. Kolb's Farm in Marietta, Georgia, was the site of a battle in 1864, in which almost 1,000 Confederate soldiers lost their lives. Many ghosts are said to still haunt the battlefield, even though buildings have been erected on the land. One ghost lives in a family's spare bedroom, but the spirit is friendly and the family have grown used to his presence.

Jefferson Davis died in 1889. His ghost is said to haunt more than one location in the South.

The Ghost of Jefferson Davis

Jefferson Davis was president of the Confederacy, which broke away from the Union in 1861. After the defeat of the Confederacy, Davis was imprisoned in Fort Monroe, off the coast of Virginia. His ghost and that of his wife, Varina, are said to live on in the fort. Another story is that Davis's spirit haunts his last home, Beauvoir, in Biloxi, Mississippi.

WHITE HOUSE GHOSTS

One of the most haunted buildings in the United States is also the most famous house in the country. The spirits of President Abraham Lincoln, First Lady Dolley Madison, and many others are said to have appeared in the White House on many occasions. All kinds of people, from presidents to staff and visitors, have reported strange apparitions and spooky noises.

The White House is said to be one of the most haunted buildings anywhere in the world.

Lincoln's Ghost

The most famous ghost to inhabit the White House is that of Abraham Lincoln. Eleanor Roosevelt recalled one evening when she was sitting in her study and her maid rushed in. She told Mrs. Roosevelt: "He's up there—sitting on the edge of the bed, taking off his shoes!" "Who's up where, taking off his shoes?" asked Mrs. Roosevelt. "Mister Lincoln!" replied the maid. Others who have seen Lincoln's ghost include First Lady Grace Coolidge and British Prime Minister Sir Winston Churchill.

Other Presences

The ghosts of the White House include some famous Americans. Thomas Jefferson is said to play his violin in the Yellow Oval Room, while First Lady Dolley Madison, wife of President James Madison, has been seen wandering around the Rose Garden, which she originally planted. Abigail Adams and her husband, the second president John Adams, were the first couple to move into 1600 Pennsylvania Avenue. Abigail Adams is still said to hang out the laundry in the East Room. When the White House was built, Washington, DC, was still a swamp and the air was often damp. The Adamses used the East Room for laundry because it was the driest part of the building.

First Lady Eleanor Roosevelt said she felt Abraham Lincoln's presence in his old bedroom at night.

Lincoln the Believer

President Lincoln was known to believe in ghosts. He attended two séances his wife, Mary Todd Lincoln, held at the White House to contact their dead son, Willie. The president also had a dream that predicted his own murder just three days before John Wilkes shot him at the theater on April 14, 1865, soon after the end of the Civil War.

A HAUNTED HOUSE

Borley Rectory in Essex was described by the Society for Psychical Research as the "most haunted house in England." For more than 70 years, the house was the location of many reported sightings of a number of spirits. Today, the rectory is everyone's idea of just how a haunted house should look.

Borley Rectory was left in ruins after a fire in 1939, when this photograph was taken. It was demolished five years later.

Borley Rectory was built in the middle of the nineteenth century on the site of an old abbey. The rectory's inhabitants reported seeing the ghost of a nun and strange happenings. Bells started ringing and objects were thrown around. According to local legend, back in the thirteenth century a monk and nun had run off together. After they were caught, the monk was hanged and the nun was walled up in her convent and left to die.

Under Investigation

In the twentieth century, the British ghost hunter and psychic investigator, Harry Price was called to the rectory to investigate. Price saw glass being smashed and stones being thrown. The resident pastor was so scared he quit. After the next pastor found writing scrawled on the walls asking for a mass to be said, he also gave up the job.

Moving In

Harry Price decided to move into the haunted rectory, and he placed an advertisement in the newspaper. It read: "Haunted House—Responsible persons of leisure and intelligence ... are invited to join a rota of observers in a year's night and day investigation of alleged haunted house in Home Counties. Printed instructions are supplied. Scientific training or ability to operate simple instruments an advantage. House situated in lonely hamlet, so own car is essential."

This advertisement launched many haunted house movies, such as *The House with a Clock in Its Walls* (2018). Harry Price was helped by a pastor, the Canon of Carlisle, who concluded that the female ghost was indeed a nun, but from the seventeenth century. The canon said she had been strangled by the owner of Borley Rectory. The hauntings and strange activities were said to come to an end only when the rectory was badly damaged by a fire in 1939.

A ghost at Borley Rectory was said to be that of a medieval nun, as imagined here, but Harry Price believed other spirits might be present.

CHAPTER 6

THE BELIEF LIVES ON

Ghosts are as popular today as ever. They are an important part of the entertainment industry, as can be seen from movies featuring hauntings, ghosts, and paranormal activity. For now, ghosts remain entirely fictional.

In the movie *Ghostbusters*, a team of paranormal investigators set up a business catching troublesome spirits.

Happy Halloween!

Ghosts and the paranormal play an important role in modern American culture. Halloween is one of the biggest dates in the calendar. Many kids and young people go trick or treating, and dressing up as their favorite ghoul is part of the fun. In Mexico and other cultures, the Day of the Dead is a similar time of celebration. It is said to be when the souls of loved ones return to Earth. They might not appear as ghosts, but the spirits are treated as living people. Relatives leave food, drink, and flowers on the tombs of loved ones.

Scary or Fun?

In the movies, ghosts are not always scary. *Casper the Friendly Ghost* was originally a TV cartoon that ran from 1945 to 1963. Lonely Casper scares people away because he is a ghost. The cartoon was so popular it was turned into a hit movie in 1995.

A lot of people enjoy being scared, and many movies feature terrifying ghosts, such as *The Woman in Black* (2012). Ghosts do not have to be frightening, however. Ghosts can be funny, as in movies such as *Beetlejuice* (1988) and *Ghostbusters* (1984). Ghosts can even be romantic. The movie *Ghost* (1990) showed a woman communicating with the ghost of her dead husband via a medium to solve his murder.

Halloween is now such a huge holiday that it is easy to forget the event is based on paying respect to the dead.

Where's the Proof?

Today, there is no shortage of information about ghosts and hauntings. There are catalogs online of all kinds of ghostly experiences. There are even cell phone and tablet apps to help people track ghosts or record strange and inexplicable happenings. There are thousands of reports of ghostly activity, and it seems that many people really want to believe that ghosts might exist. As yet, however, there is no proof.

TALKING TO THE DEAD

The late 1800s and early 1900s witnessed a craze for mediums, or people who claimed they could speak to the dead. This phenomenon was part of the wider growth of spiritualism, which is a belief that spirits inhabit the world. Sir Arthur Conan Doyle, the British author who created the detective Sherlock Holmes, was a famous spiritualist.

Believing in Spirits

Conan Doyle was a trained physician, but his medical training did not prevent him believing it was possible to contact the spirits of the dead. Having lost both his wife and son, some people argue he may have been more willing to believe the dead were still present than most people. At a séance conducted by a medium soon after the end of World War I in 1918, Conan Doyle was convinced he heard the voice of his younger son Kingsley, who had died from wounds he sustained in the conflict. He then claimed he met and embraced his own mother, whose spirit had appeared with the help of two American mediums.

Sir Arthur Conan Doyle (second from left) is shown here on vacation with his family. He tried to contact various family members after they died.

Promoting a Belief

Even after the American mediums were exposed as frauds, Conan Doyle refused to stop believing. Instead, he began touring and lecturing, showing off his collection of spirit photographs, which were a popular way to demonstrate that ghosts existed. He joined societies that researched psychic happenings, and claimed he had seen a ghost himself. No matter how much scientific evidence suggested that ghosts did not exist, Conan Doyle refused to accept it. He became one of the leading supporters of spiritualism in Britain.

Harry Houdini became interested in the occult because he wanted to contact his dead mother.

A Famous Unbeliever

On the other side of the spiritualist debate from Conan Doyle was the famous escapologist Harry Houdini. For 30 years, Houdini read everything he could find about spiritualism and attended many séances. In his book *A Magician Among The Spirits* (1924), he wrote, "In all that time I have not found one incident that savored of the genuine."

THE AMITYVILLE HOUSE

In 1975, the Lutz family moved into a house in Amityville, Long Island, New York. The previous year, the house had been the location of a mass murder in which a whole family was killed. After just a few months, the Lutz family fled their new home because of a series of terrifying paranormal events.

House of Murders

The Lutzes moved into the large house on December 18, 1975. They knew that, just a year earlier, 24-year-old Ronald DeFeo had murdered six members of his family there, but they were attracted by the house's low selling price. They believed they had a bargain—instead, after just 28 days in the house, they fled.

Ronald DeFeo claimed to have been driven to commit murder by a strange force inside the house.

Terror at Home

In that time, George Lutz and his family reported crucifixes being turned upside down and swarms of flies appearing in the middle of winter. In the basement, they found a hidden "red room," whose garish painted walls gave them nightmares about animal sacrifice. The family called in a priest, who claimed to hear a voice in an empty room shout, "Get out!" George Lutz started to suffer from hallucinations. He heard a marching band somewhere inside the house, and saw a vision of his wife as a shriveled up old hag.

After the family quit the house, psychics held a séance and declared it was home to an evil spirit. The saga was turned into a best-selling novel and a 1979 movie, both entitled *The Amityville Horror*, which made the house even more terrifying.

The movie of the Amityville haunting featured walls dripping with blood—but they were not part of the original story.

The Most Haunted Place in America

The Stanley Hotel in Estes Park, Colorado, opened in 1909. Located high in the Rocky Mountains, it failed to make any money. In 1974, a novelist and his wife checked into room 217. Weird things happened that night. The writer was Stephen King and he turned the story into one of the most famous ghost stories and movies of all time, *The Shining*.

PHOTOGRAPHING GHOSTS

In the early days of cameras, a number of people claimed to photograph the dead. The images have now been shown not to be genuine.

Ghostly Images

In 1860, New Jersey photographer W. Campbell developed a photograph of a chair that revealed a small boy sitting on it. A year later, a Boston photographer named William H. Mumler took a self-portrait. When developed, it showed a ghostly figure in the background that Mumler identified as his dead cousin. Soon Mumler had set up as a "spirit photographer," charging high fees for his images.

Mumler's most famous image showed Mary Todd Lincoln, the widow of Abraham Lincoln. In the photograph, the ghostly figure of the dead president stood behind his widow. The police charged Mumler as a swindler. At his trial, the court was shown how he created images of "spirits" by adding a second person to the negative of a photograph, leaving a ghostly shape.

Mumler's images seemed to show ghosts standing behind his living subjects.

Trick or True?

Today, anyone can repeat the kind of trick photography that resulted in the arrest of Mumler. Many smartphone cameras come with an app that allowers users to insert a ghostly image into any photograph. The app is marketed as a fun way to adapt pictures of your friends and family—but the results can be scarily convincing!

A Lasting Belief

After over a century of people claiming to photograph ghosts, the hunt for spirits continues. In the 2000s, it became the basis for a new type of television show, referred to as paranormal TV. Shows such as *Fear*, which premiered on MTV in 2000, are filmed in the style of news reports as cameras follow psychics as they investigate locations that are said to be haunted. They often report strange noises and feelings of terror, though no show has yet succeeded in filming an apparition.

The belief in ghosts remains strong, but even after centuries of research, thousands of hours of film, and many thousands of photographs, there remains no proof that ghosts exist—but also, no proof that they do not.

Many modern photographs seem to show ghosts—but are any of them genuine, or are they all just smart fakes, like this one?

TIMELINE

1091 — The priest Walchelin sees a spirit army in northern France.

1400 — A monk writes down ghost stories in Byland Abbey, England.

1600 — William Shakespeare writes the play *Hamlet*. The plot centers on the ghost of Hamlet's father.

1716 — A ghost named Old Jeffrey haunts the Old Rectory, the home of John Wesley's father.

1760s — The haunting of a house in Cock Lane, London, captures the imagination of the city.

1800s — The merchant ship *The Flying Dutchman* is said to haunt the high seas.

1817 — The Bell Witch starts to haunt the Bell family farm in Tennessee.

1818 — Mary Shelley publishes *Frankenstein*.

1843 — Charles Dickens publishes his story *A Christmas Carol*.

1840s — The Fox sisters of New York communicate with the ghost of a peddler said to have been murdered.

1865 — At the end of the Civil War, the ghosts of unburied soldiers are said to haunt the battlefields.

1861 William Mumler, later exposed as a fraud, takes his first "spirit" photograph.

1863 Borley Rectory is built. It becomes one of England's most haunted houses.

1879 The *Illustrated Police News* publishes details of the ghostly tollkeeper.

1882 The Society of Psychical Research is formed in London.

1918 Author Sir Arthur Conan Doyle becomes convinced he can talk to dead relatives via mediums and séances.

1975 A family is driven from its home in Amityville, Long Island, New York, by demonic events.

1976 The Committee for Skeptical Inquiry (CSI) is formed in New York to prove paranormal activity.

1977 The Stanley Hotel haunting is turned into a book entitled *The Shining*.

1984 *Ghostbusters* is a hit comedy movie about scientists attempting to control supernatural beings.

1990 The movie *Ghost* depicts a romance between a wife and her dead husband.

2000 Ghost-hunting show *Fear* premieres on MTV.

2012 *The Woman in Black* is a modern ghost movie based on a 1983 novel written by English author Susan Hill.

GLOSSARY

afterlife A place where the dead continue to exist.
anatomy The structure of the body.
ancestor A member of an earlier generation of a person's family.
apparitions Ghostly appearances.
ceremonies Rituals carried out as part of a religious or public occasion.
clergy People who carry out services in a church.
conjure To make a ghost appear by using a magic ritual.
corpse A dead body.
corrupt To make something impure.
crucifixes Crosses used as symbols of Jesus and Christianity.
eternity Unending time.
extra sensory perception (ESP) Getting information about the world without using the physical senses.
fictional Imaginary, made-up.
fraud A deception carried out for money or gain.
funeral A ceremony held after a person's death to dispose of the body.
hallucinations The apparent appearance of things that are not actually present.
imp A small, mischevious spirit.
mass A religious service in which people receive symbols of the body and blood of Jesus Christ.
Methodist A branch of the Protestant form of Christianity
mischief Trouble or harm.
negative A photographic image in which dark and light areas are reversed.
overseer A supervisor in charge of a group of slave workers.
parallel Describes a universe that exists alongside ours.
paranormal Describes events beyond normal scientific understanding.
peasants Poor agricultural laborers.
phenomena Things and events that can be observed.
philosopher Someone who thinks deeply about subjects, such as life.
possess To take over a person's body.
prophet In the Bible, a messenger from God.
Protestant Someone who observes the Protestant form of Christianity, which began in the 1500s.
psychical Relating to the mind.
restlessness The inability to remain still.
revenge A punishment handed out by someone who has been wronged.
rituals Ceremonies with a series of actions performed in a strict order.
sacred Holy or linked with a god.
sacrifices Offerings to the gods.
shrouded Wrapped in a garment resembling a sheet.
souls The spirits of human beings.
supernatural Not explained by science or the laws of nature.
tragedy A story that ends in death or sorrow.
vampire A corpse said to leave its grave at night to drink people's blood.
veil A thin covering.
visions Seeing things as if in a trance or dream.

FOR FURTHER READING

BOOKS

Bingham, Jane. *Ghosts and Haunted Houses: Myth or Reality* (Investigating Unsolved Mysteries). North Mankato, MN: Capstone Press, 2018.

Gagne, Tammy. *Ghosts of the White House* (Ghosts and Hauntings). North Mankato, MN: Capstone Press, 2018.

Shoup, Kate. *Ghosts, Possessions, and Unexplained Presences* (Paranormal Investigations). New York, NY: Cavendish Square Publishing, 2017.

Wood, Alix. *Creepy Cemeteries* (World's Scariest Places). New York, NY: Gareth Stevens Publishing, 2017.

WEBSITES

A Christmas Carol—*www.stormfax.com/1dickens.htm*
The complete text of Charles Dickens' famous story.

Ghost Hunting—*http://kids.ghostvillage.com*
A site for kids that explains how people hunt for signs of paranormal activity, and what they find.

Ghost Photographs—*http://mentalfloss.com/article/87784/13-historys-most-famous-ghost-photos*
A list of some famous photographs that claim to show ghosts.

Ghosts—*http://science.howstuffworks.com/science-vs-myth/afterlife/ghost.htm*
The debate about whether ghosts really exist.

INDEX